THE

AGE OF

EXPLORATION

THE
AGE OF
EXPLORATION

EDITED BY
SUSANNA KELLER

Britannica®
Educational Publishing
IN ASSOCIATION WITH
ROSEN
EDUCATIONAL SERVICES

Published in 2016 by Britannica Educational Publishing (a trademark of Encyclopædia Britannica, Inc.) in association with The Rosen Publishing Group, Inc.
29 East 21st Street, New York, NY 10010

Distributed exclusively by Rosen Publishing.
To see additional Britannica Educational Publishing titles, go to rosenpublishing.com.

First Edition

Britannica Educational Publishing
J.E. Luebering: Director, Core Reference Group
Anthony L. Green: Editor, Compton's by Britannica

Rosen Publishing
Amelie von Zumbusch: Editor
Nelson Sá: Art Director
Michael Moy: Designer
Cindy Reiman: Photography Manager
Bruce Donnola: Photo Researcher

Library of Congress Cataloging-in-Publication Data

Keller, Susanna.
The Age of Exploration / edited by Susanna Keller. — First edition.
    pages cm. — (Early American History)
Includes bibliographical references and index.
ISBN 978-1-68048-267-6 (library bound)
1. America—Discovery and exploration—Juvenile literature. I. Title.
E101.K45 2016
970.01—dc23

                                                                2015016290

Manufactured in the United States

Photo Credits: Cover, p. 3 SuperStock/Getty Images; pp. 6-7 The Art Archive/SuperStock; pp. 9, 12, 19, 53, 61 Encyclopaedia Britannica, Inc.; pp. 14-15 Private Collection/Index/Bridgeman Images; p. 17 Ann Ronan Picture Library/Heritage-Images; p. 21 Alinari/Art Resource, New York; pp. 26-27 ACME Imagery/SuperStock; p. 30 "Spanish Explorers in the Southern United States, 1528-1543" edited by Frederick W. Hodge; pp. 32-33 Architect of the Capitol; pp. 35, 38, 66-67 Library of Congress Prints and Photographs Division Washington, D.C.; pp. 36-37 MPI/Archive Photos/Getty Images; pp. 42-43 Time Life Pictures/The LIFE Picture Collection/Getty Images; pp. 46-47 Château de Versailles, France/Bridgeman Images; p. 49 DEA Picture Library/Getty Images; p. 50 Universal History Archive/Universal Images Group/Getty Images; p. 55 New York Daily News Archive/Getty Images; p. 56 Print Collector/Hulton Archive/Getty Images; p. 58 Karl Maslowski; p. 60 Archive Photos/Getty Images; p. 64 Interim Archive/Archive Photos/Getty Images

CONTENTS

The first peoples to explore and settle the Americas were the ancestors of the American Indians. These early explorers were members of nomadic hunter-gatherer cultural groups. They moved from Asia to North America during the last ice age, when thick ice sheets covered much of northern North America. As the ice sheets absorbed water, sea levels dropped and a land bridge emerged along what is now the Bering Strait. From about 30,000 to 12,000 years ago, this land bridge connected northeastern Asia to what is now Alaska. Some peoples came to North America by following the Pacific coast southward. They may have combined walking with boat travel. Others walked across a glacier-free area through the center of what is now Canada.

Continued melting of the ice gradually opened up the land, allowing people to spread out across North America and into South America. No single person made any large part of the long journey; one group after another continued the march over many centuries. The first Europeans did not arrive in the

Scientists call the now-underwater stretch of land that the ancestors of the American Indians crossed the Bering Land Bridge. This image by a modern artist shows a group of hunter-gatherers crossing it.

Americas until many thousands of years later. By that time, the Indians had explored and settled all portions of what the Europeans would call the "New World."

Europeans "rediscovered" the Americas during the period of maritime exploration known as the Age of Exploration, which began in the late 15th century. During this period, Europeans also explored the coasts of Africa, sent ships directly to India and Southeast Asia, and sailed around the globe. European exploration ushered in globalization— the development of economic and cultural links throughout the world. Europeans conquered and colonized distant lands, establishing vast empires. In the Americas, violent conquest and diseases accidentally brought over by the Europeans killed enormous numbers of Indians. Smallpox, yellow fever, malaria, influenza, and measles were among the diseases spread to the New World. Indian populations further decreased as Europeans forced them to work on plantations and in mines under harsh conditions. Europeans later imported African slaves to replace the Indians as a labor source. Meanwhile, gold and silver poured back to Europe from the mines, enriching European economies.

European exploration led to the exchange of plants, animals, germs, technologies, and ideas across continents, in what is now called the Columbian Exchange (after Christopher Columbus). Potatoes, corn, tomatoes, sweet potatoes, squash, cassava,

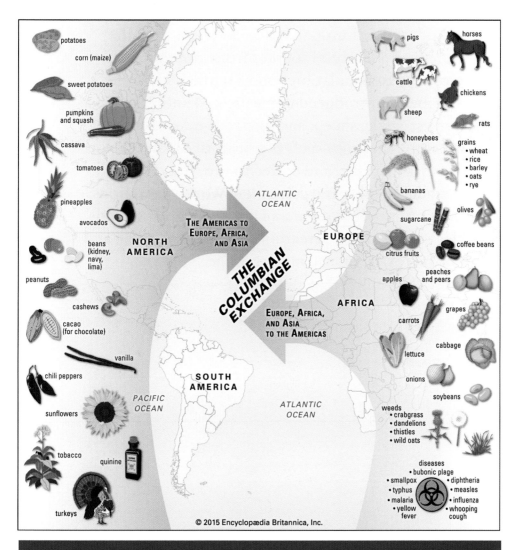

potatoes

corn (maize)

sweet potatoes

pumpkins and squash

cassava

tomatoes

pineapples

avocados

beans (kidney, navy, lima)

NORTH AMERICA

peanuts

cashews

cacao (for chocolate)

vanilla

chili peppers

PACIFIC OCEAN

sunflowers

tobacco

quinine

turkeys

SOUTH AMERICA

ATLANTIC OCEAN

THE AMERICAS TO EUROPE, AFRICA, AND ASIA

THE COLUMBIAN EXCHANGE

EUROPE, AFRICA, AND ASIA TO THE AMERICAS

EUROPE

AFRICA

pigs

horses

cattle

chickens

sheep

rats

honeybees

grains
• wheat
• rice
• barley
• oats
• rye

bananas

olives

sugarcane

coffee beans

citrus fruits

apples

peaches and pears

grapes

carrots

cabbage

lettuce

onions

soybeans

weeds
• crabgrass
• dandelions
• thistles
• wild oats

diseases
• bubonic plage
• smallpox
• typhus
• malaria
• yellow fever
• diphtheria
• measles
• influenza
• whooping cough

© 2015 Encyclopædia Britannica, Inc.

In the Columbian Exchange, numerous plants, animals, and microbes from Europe, Asia, and Africa were introduced to the Americas, and numerous others were transferred from the Americas to Europe, Asia, and Africa.

cacao (the source of chocolate), hot peppers, peanuts, pineapple, and tobacco were among the crops
introduced to Europe, Africa, and Asia from the
Americas. New food sources from more productive
crops led to population booms in the Old World.
Europeans introduced domesticated animals such as
horses, cattle, sheep, and pigs to the Americas. They
also brought crops such as wheat, rice, oats, bananas,
olives, sugarcane, and coffee to the Americas and
introduced steel and guns. New World plantations
began to produce sugar and cotton in great quanti-
ties, leading to the creation of sugar processing and
cotton textile industries in Europe.

CHAPTER ONE

DISCOVERING THE NEW WORLD

E uropean explorers found the New World by mistake; they were not looking to find new continents but new sea routes. Europeans mainly wanted to find better trade routes to China, India, and Southeast Asia. They valued many products from Asia, including cloves, pepper, and other spices that were used to make food taste good and to keep it from spoiling. Also in demand were such luxuries as sheer, colorful silken cloths, rich carpets, and sparkling jewelry.

The wealth of the East had been trickling into western Europe mainly by overland routes. Asian merchandise was thus both scarce and expensive in Europe. Goods changed hands many times before they reached the consumer, and at each exchange the cost increased. Merchandise was transported by camel or horse caravans, with each animal carrying only a comparatively small load. Ships could carry goods more cheaply and in greater quantity. The Italian port cities were

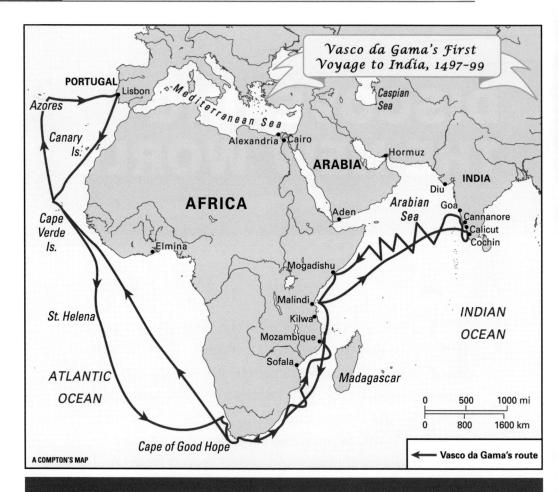

Vasco da Gama's First
Voyage to India, 1497–99

PORTUGAL
Lisbon
Azores
Mediterranean Sea
Caspian Sea
Canary Is.
Alexandria · Cairo
Hormuz
ARABIA
INDIA
Diu
AFRICA
Arabian Sea
Goa
Cape Verde Is.
Aden
Cannanore
Elmina
Calicut
Cochin
Mogadishu
St. Helena
Malindi
Kilwa
INDIAN OCEAN
Mozambique
ATLANTIC OCEAN
Sofala
Madagascar
0   500   1000 mi
0   800   1600 km
Cape of Good Hope
A COMPTON'S MAP
← Vasco da Gama's route

In 1497–98 the Portuguese explorer Vasco da Gama's ships rounded the Cape of Good Hope and reached India by sea, successfully finding the eastern route to Asia.

satisfied with their monopoly of the old trading routes. However, Portugal, Spain, England, and France wanted to find new sea routes to Asia in order to import goods directly. In the late 15th century, Portuguese explorers pioneered the eastern route to Asia by sailing around the southern tip of Africa.

THE VIKINGS

The Vikings of Norway are the first Europeans known to have visited North America. However, people in the rest of Europe were not aware of these discoveries. A Viking named Gunnbjörn Ulfsson sailed near Greenland in the 10th century, and Erik the Red was the first to colonize the island. The first Europeans to land on the North American mainland were the Viking explorer Leif Eriksson and his party. They are believed to have reached the coasts of Newfoundland and Labrador (now in northeastern Canada) in 1001. Archaeologists have found evidence of Viking settlements there from about Leif's time.

COLUMBUS

By the 1490s educated people knew that the world was round and that the east could be reached by sailing west. To believe, however, that it would be practical to make such a voyage was a different matter. Master navigator Christopher Columbus was one of the most optimistic advocates of the western route. In 1492 he set off on a voyage to find this route.

Columbus's expedition had three ships. The *Niña* and the *Pinta* were small, speedy ships called caravels.

On Columbus's voyage of 1492–93, Vicente Pinzón commanded the *Niña*, while his brother Martín Pinzón was captain of the *Pinta*. Columbus commanded the *Santa María*, the flagship. This 19th-century print shows the three ships.

Columbus's flagship, the *Santa María*, was more than twice the size of the caravels. Funding for the voyage came from the Spanish monarchs Ferdinand and Isabella as well a group of Italian bankers in Seville, Spain.

The little fleet set sail from Palos, Spain, on August 3, 1492. For the most part the passage was smooth and the winds were steady. As the days passed, however, the men could not see how they would sail home against winds that had blown them steadily west. By October 9 the men were ready to rebel. Columbus said that he would turn back if land was not sighted within three days. On the night of October 11, Columbus thought he saw lights in the distance. At 2 AM on October 12, Rodrigo de Triana, a seaman aboard the *Pinta*, cried loudly the first sight of land.

The small Spanish fleet had unknowingly reached not Asia but the Caribbean islands that are now The Bahamas. The islands are part of North America, lying between

Florida and Cuba. Columbus named the first land that the expedition sighted San Salvador. This island may have been the one now called San Salvador or perhaps Samana Cay. The expedition landed and was met by a group of Taino people. Carrying the royal banners of Ferdinand and Isabella, the Spaniards took possession of San Salvador for Spain.

The Taino were friendly and helpful to the Spaniards. Columbus believed that he had reached the "Indies"—East and Southeast Asia. He thus called the people he encountered there Indians. The Caribbean islands are today known as the West Indies, to distinguish them from the East Indies of Asia.

Sailing on with Indian guides, Columbus explored several islands. Everywhere the Spaniards asked where gold could be found. On December 6, 1492, the explorers reached an island called Ayti (Haiti) by its Taino inhabitants. Columbus renamed the island Hispaniola. Previously he had found small trinkets of gold, but on Hispaniola he found enough gold to save him from ridicule on his return to Spain. On December 25 the *Santa María* ran aground off the north coast of Hispaniola and had to be abandoned. From its timber Columbus built a small fort, La Navidad, with the help of a Taino chief named Guacanagarí. The Spaniards left 39 crewmen behind at La Navidad as colonists.

On January 16, 1493, the *Niña* and the *Pinta* began the return voyage. They carried gold, colorful parrots,

After his return to Europe in 1493, Columbus made three more trips to the New World: 1493 to 1496, 1498 to 1500, and 1502 to 1504. To the day he died, however, he still believed that he had reached Asia.

other strange animals and plants, spices, and some Indian cloth and ornaments. They also carried several Indians, whom they had captured to show to Ferdinand and Isabella. The journey back was a nightmare. A terrible storm engulfed the fleet, and the ships were separated. The *Pinta* made port at the Spanish town of Bayona, to the north of Portugal. Columbus, on the *Niña*, made it back to Palos on March 15, 1493.

THE LINE OF DEMARCATION

When Columbus returned to Spain, the Portuguese claimed that he had merely visited a part of their dominion of Guinea in Africa. Spain and Portugal asked the pope to settle the dispute. He complied in 1493 by drawing an arbitrary north-south Line of Demarcation. The line was redrawn the following year. Spain was given exclusive rights to all newly discovered and undiscovered lands west of the line. Portuguese expeditions were to keep to the east of the line. However, no other European country facing the Atlantic ever accepted this line.

The Line of Demarcation allowed Portugal to claim a significant prize in the New World—Brazil. On March 9, 1500, the Portuguese navigator Pedro Álvares Cabral set sail from Lisbon for India, intending to follow the route around Africa that Vasco da

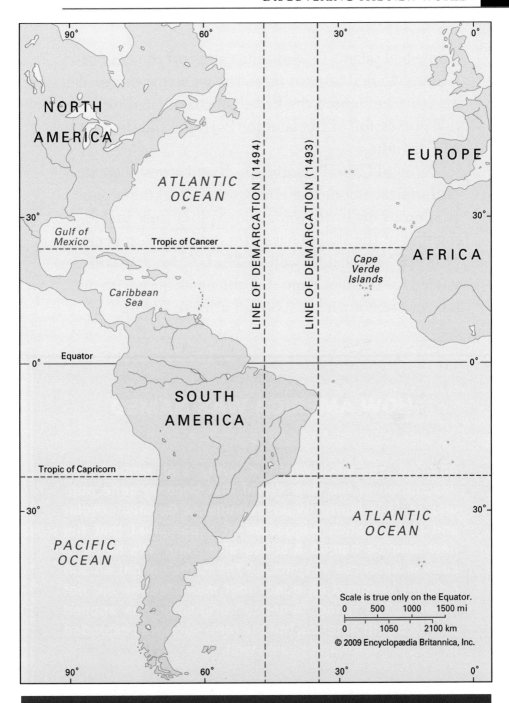

The Line of Demarcation between Spanish and Portuguese territory was first defined by Pope Alexander VI (1493) and was later revised by the Treaty of Tordesillas (1494).

Gama had taken. To avoid the calms off the Gulf of Guinea, Cabral bore so far to the west that on April 22, 1500, he sighted the Brazilian coast. He took formal possession of the land for Portugal and then set off for India.

News of Cabral's landing in Brazil aroused great enthusiasm among the Portuguese. The king began to sponsor major transatlantic explorations, including that of the Italian navigator Amerigo Vespucci in 1501–02. Vespucci, as well as scholars, became convinced for the first time that the newly discovered lands were not part of Asia but a "New World."

HOW AMERICA WAS NAMED

Amerigo Vespucci wrote a lively and embellished description of the New World that became quite popular. In 1507 Martin Waldseemüller, a German scholar and cartographer, suggested in a pamphlet that the new land be named America after him. (His name in Latin is Americus Vespucius.) The name caught on and brought Vespucci an honor that many feel he did not deserve. The name "America" originally was applied only to South America, but the term soon was extended to include North America as well.

AMERICVS VESPVCCI

The merchant and explorer-navigator Amerigo Vespucci took part in two important expeditions to the New World (1499–1500, 1501–02). This portrait of him is now in the Uffizi Gallery, in Florence, Italy.

MAGELLAN

A Portuguese captain named Ferdinand Magellan believed there might be a water passage through South America that would lead to Asia. He presented his idea to the king of Spain, Charles I. Magellan convinced the king that the richest lands in the East—including the Spice Islands (now the Moluccas of Indonesia)—lay in the region reserved for Spain by the Line of Demarcation. The king commissioned Magellan to find a western route to Asia.

Spanish officials furnished five small ships for the expedition. Magellan's flagship, the *Trinidad*, had as consorts the *San Antonio*, the *Concepción*, the *Victoria*, and the *Santiago*. They carried a crew of about 250 men, mostly Spaniards. The fleet left Sanlúcar de Barrameda, in southwestern Spain, on September 20, 1519.

The ships sailed across the Atlantic Ocean and down the coast of South America in search of a strait leading to the Pacific Ocean. After spending a difficult winter in what is now Argentina, they finally found a strait leading westward on October 21, 1520. This channel, now named the Strait of Magellan, lies between the southern tip of mainland South America and the island of Tierra del Fuego. The voyage through the strait proved to be an extremely difficult one. The channel was long, deep, tortuous, rock-walled, and bedeviled by icy squalls and dense fogs. After 38 days, the ships sailed out into the open ocean. At the news that the ocean had been sighted, the iron-willed Magellan reportedly broke down and cried with joy.

Once away from land, the ocean seemed calm enough. Magellan named it the Pacific, meaning "peaceable." However, the ocean proved to be vast. For 14 weeks the little ships sailed without encountering land. Short of food and water, the sailors ate sawdust mixed with putrid ship's biscuits and what few rats they could catch. On March 6, 1521, exhausted and in poor health, they landed at the island of Guam. They were the first Europeans to have crossed the Pacific.

They left a few days later, sailing toward the Philippines. There, Magellan secured the first alliance for Spain with a leader in the Pacific. At Cebu Island the expedition converted the island's ruler to Christianity. Weeks later, however, Magellan was killed in a fight with the people of Mactan Island.

The survivors, in two ships, sailed on to the Moluccas, where the expedition obtained valuable spices. One ship attempted, but failed, to return across the Pacific. The remaining ship, the *Victoria*, sailed alone across the Indian Ocean. It was commanded by the Spanish navigator Juan Sebastián del Cano. The ship rounded the Cape of Good Hope and arrived at Seville on September 9, 1522. After a voyage of slightly more than three years, it had circled the globe. Besides Cano, the surviving crew consisted of only 17 Europeans and a small number of Moluccans.

The expedition confirmed the idea that Earth is round and demonstrated the vastness of the Pacific Ocean. It also proved that Columbus had discovered not the route to China but rather a New World.

CHAPTER TWO

EXPLORING THE SOUTH AND SOUTHWEST

According to the Line of Demarcation, Spain was left in control of most of the New World. Spanish conquerors, known as conquistadores, soon began to explore and take control of the region that is now Latin America. The first European attempts to explore the southern and southwestern regions of what is now the United States were expeditions that set off from the Spanish colonies in Mexico and the Caribbean.

PONCE DE LEÓN

The first European known to have visited what is now the U.S. mainland was the Spanish explorer Juan Ponce de León. While serving as governor of eastern Hispaniola, he had heard persistent reports that there was gold to be found on Puerto Rico. In 1508–09 he explored and settled that island. He founded the colony's oldest settlement, Caparra, near what is now San Juan.

The Spanish king encouraged Ponce de León to continue searching for new lands. The explorer learned from Indians of an island called Bimini (in The Bahamas) where there was said to be a miraculous spring or fountain that kept those who drank from it perpetually young. In search of this "fountain of youth," he led an expedition from Puerto Rico in March 1513. Although he never found the fabled fountain, he was the first European to encounter the ocean current known as the Gulf Stream. He was also the first to sight what is now Florida. In April he landed on Florida's coast, near the site of what is today St. Augustine. He

Ponce de León landed in Florida on Easter. He named the land to commemorate the holiday (in Spanish, *Pascua florida*) or, possibly, for the flowers he found growing everywhere. (*Florida* also means "flowery.")

did not realize that he was on the mainland of North America but supposed that he had landed on an island.

Ponce de León claimed this land for Spain. He then coasted southward, sailing through the Florida Keys. He ended his search near Charlotte Harbor on Florida's west coast. He returned to Florida in 1521 to build a settlement, but he was slain by Indians.

NARVÁEZ AND CABEZA DE VACA

Additional Spanish expeditions to colonize the region followed. The king gave Spanish conquistador Panfilo de Narváez authorization to subdue and colonize vast lands from Florida westward. He sailed from Spain on June 17, 1527, with five ships and about 600 soldiers, sailors, and colonists. He began to suffer losses early on. In Santo Domingo 140 men deserted the expedition. In Cuba a hurricane sank two of the ships, killing 50 men and several horses.

Narváez remained in Cuba until late February 1528. He then sailed with five ships and 400 followers to the region around Tampa Bay in Florida. He sent the ships north and began an overland expedition in May with about 300 men. The force made a difficult and distressing march northward, continually fighting Indians. Near the end of July, the survivors reached the area around what is now St. Marks, in Florida's panhandle region.

Narváez had expected to meet his ships on the coast, but they did not arrive. Instead, the expedition's suffering survivors had to build five new ships themselves. In late September the 245 surviving men sailed along the coast, hoping to reach Mexico. The ships drifted along the northern part of the Gulf of Mexico, passing Pensacola Bay and the mouth of the Mississippi River. As the journey progressed, ships were gradually lost. In about early November 1528 Narváez disappeared when his own vessel was suddenly blown out to sea.

One of the vessels, commanded by Álvar Núñez Cabeza de Vaca, reached the shore near what is now Galveston, Texas. There, he and his men met survivors of two of the other ships. Of all these men, only 15 were still alive by the following spring. Eventually only Cabeza de Vaca and three others remained. Among these survivors was a slave named Estéban, who was the first black man known to have entered Florida.

In the following years Cabeza de Vaca and his companions spent much time among various Indian tribes. The survivors eventually crossed the Rio Grande river and turned south. Though they found only the gravest hardship and poverty during their wanderings, the men made their way back to Mexico in 1536, some eight years after they had set out.

Although only four men returned from the disastrous expedition, they had been among the first Europeans to see the mouth of the Mississippi River.

Cabeza de Vaca wrote a detailed account of his travels. It was called *La Relación* (The Account) when it was first published in 1542, but later editions were known as *Naufragios* (Shipwrecks).

The men returned with stories of rich Indian civilizations that supposedly existed somewhere in the north. There were said to be seven "cities of gold," called the Seven Cities of Cíbola.

DE SOTO

In April 1538 Hernando de Soto set off to search for gold in the region. He and his men did not find riches, but they became the first Europeans to travel on the Mississippi River. De Soto is often credited with being the European discoverer of the river, though other explorers had already seen its mouth.

De Soto had earlier participated in the Spanish conquests of Central America and Peru. He sailed on this expedition from Spain in command of 10 ships and 700 men. After a brief stop in Cuba, the expedition landed in May 1539 on the coast of Florida. After spending the winter at a small Indian village, de Soto and his men traveled to the north and west. They passed through Georgia, the Carolinas, and Tennessee. Along the way they met many Indian tribes. De Soto forced the Indians to furnish supplies and tortured their chiefs in a useless effort to make them tell where gold was hidden. They also abducted Indians to serve as their guides. This brutality led to many battles.

Although de Soto and his men did not find gold, they obtained an assortment of pearls. They turned southward into Alabama and headed toward Mobile Bay, where they expected to meet their ships. However, at a fortified Indian town, a confederation of Indians attacked the Spaniards. The Indians were decimated. The Spanish were also severely crippled, losing most of their equipment and all their pearls.

After a month's rest, de Soto decided to turn north again and head inland in search of treasure. This decision was to prove disastrous. Moving northwest through Alabama and then west through Mississippi, de Soto's party was attacked relentlessly by Indians. On May 21, 1541, the Spaniards saw for the first time the Mississippi River, south of Memphis, Tennessee. The explorers built boats and crossed the river. They then made their way through Arkansas and Louisiana. Everywhere de Soto searched, the Indians reported gold "just ahead" in order to escape his torture. After three years, he still had found no gold.

The expedition turned back to the Mississippi River early in 1542. Overcome by fever, de Soto died in Louisiana, and his comrades buried his body in the Mississippi. By this

William H. Powell's 1853 painting *Discovery of the Mississippi* shows the de Soto expedition's discovery of the Mississippi River. Hernando de Soto is the figure on horseback at the center of the image.

time, only about half of the original party remained. Luis de Moscoso led the expedition's survivors down the Mississippi on rafts. They reached Mexico in 1543.

CORONADO

Meanwhile, the Spanish leader of New Spain—which included Mexico, Central America, and the Caribbean—had sent out an expedition in 1539. Its mission was to locate the wealthy Seven Cities of Cíbola. The expedition was led by Marcos de Niza (or Fray Marcos), a Franciscan priest. The expedition's guide was Estéban, the black slave who had been shipwrecked with Cabeza de Vaca. The men journeyed northward from Mexico, across the desert to Arizona. Niza sent Estéban ahead to scout the area. He soon learned that Estéban had been killed by Indians. Niza continued on until he reportedly saw the Seven Cities of Cíbola in the distance. He had perhaps actually seen the pueblos, or towns, of the Zuni Indians in New Mexico. In any case, Niza did not visit the cities but returned to Mexico with tales of riches.

Niza's report of great wealth stirred interest in further exploration of the region. The leader of New Spain sent forth a large military expedition, led by Francisco Vázquez de Coronado, to conquer the fabled cities. Niza served as its guide. The expedition consisted of some 300 Spaniards, hundreds of Indian allies and Indian slaves, horses, and herds of sheep, pigs, and cattle. Two ships under the command of Hernando

The pueblo of the Zuni people of New Mexico is believed to have inspired the legend of the Seven Cities of Cíbola. The pueblo is shown here in a 1903 photograph.

de Alarcón also sailed up the Gulf of California. This branch of the expedition discovered the mouth of the Colorado River.

The main force under Coronado departed in February 1540, traveling up the west coast of Mexico to Culiacán. A smaller unit rode north from there. The explorers encountered the Zuni towns but found no great wealth or treasure. Another scouting party, led by García López de Cárdenas, journeyed to the west. He

and his men became the first Europeans to view the
Grand Canyon of Arizona.

The expedition spent the winter in the valley of the
Rio Grande in New Mexico. New hope came from a

Francisco Vázquez de Coronado, right, leads an expedition to find the legendary
Seven Cities of Cíbola.

Plains Indian slave, whom the Spaniards called "the Turk." He told of a land to the northeast called Quivira that was very rich. With 30 men and the Turk as guide, Coronado set forth. After months they found Quivira in what is now central Kansas, but it held only Indian tepees, not gold. Coronado had the Turk executed.

The expedition returned to the Rio Grande. After wintering there, the men started homeward. The tattered army followed a route over deserts and mountains in blazing summer heat. In the fall of 1542 Coronado led only about 100 men into Mexico City. The remaining survivors trailed in during the next months. Coronado's expensive expedition had failed to find cities of gold. He had, however, established the basis for Spain's later claim to what is now the U.S. Southwest.

EXPLORING CALIFORNIA

In 1539 Spanish explorer Francisco de Ulloa led a seaward expedition to find the fabled cities of gold. He sailed along the Pacific coast of Mexico and explored the Gulf of California. Sailing around Baja California (now part of Mexico), he proved that it is a peninsula, not an island as had been thought. According to some sources, Ulloa may have continued northward and sighted California.

The first European known to have reached California was Juan Rodríguez Cabrillo. It is not known

This statue in San Diego honors Juan Rodríguez Cabrillo, the first European known to explore California.

for certain whether he was Spanish or Portuguese. In any event, he explored in the service of Spain. It is thought that Cabrillo embarked from the Mexican port of Navidad in June 1542. He explored most of the coast of California and entered San Diego and Monterey bays.

Spain's claim to California was strengthened in 1602 by the Spanish navigator Sebastián Vizcaíno, who charted the coast. He sailed from Mexico to the California coast, naming San Diego, Santa Catalina

DRAKE IN CALIFORNIA

Between 1577 and 1580 the English navigator Sir Francis Drake made a voyage around the world, with the secret financial support of Queen Elizabeth I. The English hoped to end the Spanish monopoly of the profitable trade in the Pacific. Drake sailed across the Atlantic, through the Strait of Magellan, at the southern tip of South America, and up the coast. He plundered Spanish settlements in Chile and Peru and captured treasure ships bound for Panama.

In 1579 Drake sailed up the California coast beyond San Francisco Bay and claimed the land for England. To avoid meeting the angered Spaniards on his way home, he returned to England by way of the Pacific and Indian oceans.

Island, Santa Barbara, and Monterey. He ultimately reached the Oregon coast.

The Spaniards did not launch many more expeditions to the region. Having found no cities of gold or other sources of great wealth, they did not care to explore further the disappointing lands north of Mexico. Spanish missionaries and settlers later established colonies in the areas already explored, in Florida, the Southwest, and California. However, most of Spain's colonial efforts were concentrated on exploiting the great riches already found in Mexico and South America.

CHAPTER THREE

EXPLORING THE NORTHEAST

While Spain explored the south, the French, English, and Dutch approached North America from the east. They were mostly interested in finding the Northwest Passage, a sea route to Asia through northern North America. While Roald Amundsen would eventually sail through the passage in 1905, all earlier expeditions met with failure, and many with disaster. They nevertheless made valuable explorations in what are now the northeastern United States and Canada.

CABOT

Shortly after Columbus reached the New World, King Henry VII of England authorized John Cabot (as the Italian explorer Giovanni Caboto is known in English) to sail west in search of unknown lands. In 1496 Cabot left Bristol, England, with one ship. He was soon forced to turn back, however, because of poor weather, a shortage of food, and disputes with his crew. In May 1497 he tried again. He set sail from Bristol in the small ship *Matthew* with a crew of 18 men. He proceeded around Ireland and then to the north and west, making landfall on the morning of June 24. The site of his landfall is believed to have been in what is now southern Labrador, Cape Breton Island, or Newfoundland, in eastern Canada. On going ashore, Cabot noticed signs that the area was inhabited, but he saw no people. He took possession of the land for the English king and explored the coastline by ship before returning with news of his discovery. Cabot arrived back in England on August 6, 1497, believing that he had reached the northeast coast of Asia.

The following year Cabot set out on another voyage, probably with five ships and 200 men. This time he hoped to find Japan. Cabot was never seen again. Some evidence suggests that he may have reached North America, but he was likely lost at sea.

John Cabot, his son Sebastian, and the rest of his crew prepare to set sail on England's first voyage to North America in May 1497.

Cabot's successful voyage helped lay the groundwork for the later English claim to Canada. He also demonstrated that it was possible to sail across the North Atlantic. This would prove important in the establishment of English colonies in North America. Moreover, Cabot discovered that the northwest Atlantic waters were teeming with fish. Soon Portuguese, Spanish, French, and English fishing crews braved the Atlantic crossing to fish in the waters of the Grand Banks, southeast of Newfoundland. Some fishers began to land on the coast of Newfoundland to dry their catch before returning to Europe. This fishing ushered in the initial period of contact between the Europeans and the Indians of northern North America. Although each was deeply suspicious of the other, they traded now and then in scattered locations.

VERRAZZANO AND CARTIER

France soon began establishing its claim to northern North America. Spain and France were at war, and Francis I, king of France, wanted a share of the Asian trade to finance his armies. He sent the Italian navigator Giovanni da Verrazzano to find a passage to Asia. In 1524 Verrazzano reached the American coast at what is now North Carolina and sailed north to Newfoundland. He made several discoveries on the voyage, including New York Harbor, Block Island, and Narragansett Bay. Verrazzano's report to the king contained the

PORTUGUESE AND SPANISH EXPLORERS IN THE NORTHEAST

In 1524–25 a Portuguese sea captain named Estevão Gomes (or Esteban Gómez), serving the king of Spain, explored the coast of North America from Maine to New Jersey. His descriptions suggested that there was little mineral wealth there and led the Spaniards to consider this region far less valuable than the lands they had in the south. Thus they ignored the greater part of the eastern coast of North America.

The Portuguese made one important discovery in this northern region. In 1501 Gaspar Côrte-Real reached Newfoundland. His voyages were not repeated, though, as Portugal soon needed all of its resources to develop its East India empire and its colony in Brazil.

first description of the northeastern coast of North America. It also gave France its first claim to American lands by right of discovery.

King Francis I decided to send another expedition to explore the northern lands in the hope of discovering a passage to Asia. The explorer Jacques Cartier set off from France on April 20, 1534, with two ships and 61 men. He reached North America a few weeks later. Cartier traveled along the west coast of Newfoundland and discovered Prince Edward Island. He explored the Gulf of St. Lawrence as far as Anticosti Island, claiming the shores of the gulf for the French king. He took two Indians with him on the journey back to France.

Cartier returned the following year to explore further. Guided by the two Indians he had brought back, Cartier sailed up the St. Lawrence River as far as what is now Quebec city. He established a base and proceeded with a small party as far as the island of Montreal. Cartier was welcomed by the local Iroquois Indians. He learned from them that two rivers led farther west to lands where gold, silver, copper, and spices abounded.

The severity of the winter came as a terrible shock. Scurvy claimed 25 of Cartier's men. To make matters worse, the explorers earned the ill will of the Iroquois. In May, as soon as the river was free of ice, the explorers seized some of the Iroquois chiefs and sailed for France. Cartier was able to report only that great riches lay farther in the interior and that a great river possibly led to Asia.

War in Europe prevented Francis I from sending another expedition until 1541. Concerned about Spanish claims to the Americas, he commissioned a nobleman, Jean-François de La Rocque de Roberval, to establish a colony in the lands discovered by Cartier. Roberval led the expedition, and Cartier served under him. Cartier sailed first, arriving at what is now Quebec city on August 23. Roberval was delayed until the following year.

The winter at Cartier's new base above Quebec proved as severe as the earlier one. He had trouble

Jacques Cartier, the first European to sail up the St. Lawrence River, explored much of eastern Canada and claimed it for France. French heritage in the region is still strong; 80 percent of people in the province of Quebec are native French speakers.

controlling his men, and their actions again aroused the hostility of the local Indians. But they found what appeared to be gold and diamonds in abundance. In the spring Cartier abandoned the base and sailed for France. There, his gold and diamonds were found to be worthless — they were really fool's gold (pyrite) and quartz. "False as a Canadian diamond" became a common French expression. Roberval enjoyed no better success. After one winter he abandoned the plan to found a colony and returned to France.

French disappointment at these meager results was great. France lost interest in these new lands for more than half a century. Nevertheless, Cartier had made the European discovery of the St. Lawrence River, which was later to become France's great entranceway into North America. He also is credited with naming Canada, from the Huron-Iroquois word *kanata*, meaning a village or settlement. (Cartier used the name to refer only to the area around Quebec city.) Moreover, the French claim to the land remained; it had only to be made good by actual settlement.

ENGLISH COLONIZATION ATTEMPTS

After John Cabot's early voyages, English explorers did not return to the New World until the late 16th century. In 1576–78 the English mariner Martin Frobisher undertook three voyages in search of the Northwest Passage to Asia. He explored Canada's northeast coast and discovered the bay near Baffin Island that now bears his name. However, his single-minded pursuit of gold limited the exploratory value of his voyages.

Sir Humphrey Gilbert, an English soldier and navigator, wrote a paper about the Northwest Passage in 1566 that later inspired many explorers to search for the elusive route to Asia. He set sail with seven ships on November 19, 1578, but his ill-equipped, badly disciplined force quickly broke up. By the spring some of the ships had drifted to England while others had turned to piracy.

Gilbert later undertook a more ambitious attempt to establish an English colony in North America. He sailed from Plymouth, England, on June 11, 1583. On August 3 he arrived at what is now St. John's, Newfoundland, which he

Sir Martin Frobisher's explorations of northeastern Canada were not very successful because he was mainly interested in looking for gold.

AETATIS SVÆ
AN 1588

AMOR ET VIRTUTE

Sir Walter Raleigh was a politician and poet, soldier and sailor, explorer and historian. His principal claim to fame, however, rests on his efforts to colonize the New World.

claimed in the name of the queen. Sailing southward with three ships, he lost the largest of them on August 29. Two days later he turned homeward. Gilbert was last seen during a great storm in the Atlantic, shouting to his companion vessel, "We are as near heaven by sea as by land." Gilbert's ship was then swallowed by the sea.

With the failure of Gilbert's voyage, the English turned to Sir Walter Raleigh to advance their fortunes in the New World. They also tried a new strategy—taking a southern rather than a northern route to North America. Raleigh sponsored attempts in the 1580s to found a permanent colony off the coast of Virginia. Although his efforts finally failed with the mysterious destruction of the Roanoke Island colony in 1587, they awakened popular interest in a permanent colonizing venture. The English established their first permanent colony in the New World—Jamestown—in Virginia in 1607.

CHAMPLAIN

French fishing fleets had continued to make almost yearly visits to the eastern shores of Canada. Chiefly as a sideline of the fishing industry, there continued an unorganized trade in furs. In Europe new methods of processing furs developed, and beaver hats in particular grew very fashionable. Thus new encouragement was given to the fur trade in Canada.

In 1604 Pierre du Gua received a French royal monopoly that gave him the exclusive right to this fur trade. That year he led his first colonizing expedition to Acadia, a region surrounding the Bay of Fundy on the eastern seaboard of Canada. Among the expedition's lieutenants was Samuel de Champlain, a geographer, navigator, and soldier.

Champlain spent three winters in Acadia. During the first winter the settlers stayed on an island in the St. Croix River. Scurvy killed nearly half the party. The second and third winters, at Annapolis Basin, claimed the lives of fewer men. During the summers Champlain searched for an ideal site for colonization. He carried out a major exploration of the northeastern coastline of what is now the United States, journeying down the Atlantic coast southward to Massachusetts Bay and beyond. He mapped in detail the harbors that his English rivals had only touched.

In 1608 Champlain was granted permission to undertake another expedition. He led a group of settlers to a site on the St. Lawrence River where they hoped to establish a center for controlling the fur trade. There he founded Quebec city and made friends of the Huron people of the region. In 1609 he went with the Huron to fight the Iroquois in New York. During this time he discovered Lake Champlain, which he named after himself. Not far from the lake he routed the Iroquois enemy with gunfire. Thereafter the Iroquois were bitter enemies of the French. Champlain later made several exploring trips in search of rivers that might lead to the Pacific Ocean. In 1615 he reached Georgian Bay and Lake Huron.

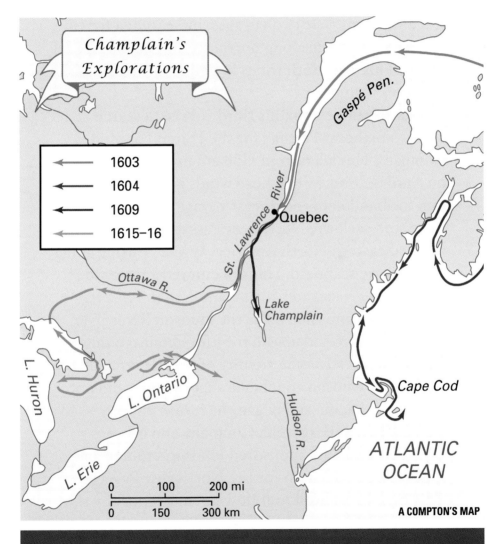

Map of Samuel de Champlain's explorations of North America in the early 17th century.

HUDSON

The English explorer Henry Hudson tried to discover a short route from Europe to Asia by sailing both northwest and northeast through the Arctic Ocean. On his first two voyages, he searched for the Northeast Passage along northern Europe, but ice blocked his way. Both times he sailed for the English Muscovy Company.

Hudson undertook his third voyage in search of the Northeast Passage for the Dutch East India Company. He sailed from Holland in the *Half Moon* on April 6, 1609. When head winds and storms forced him to abandon his northeast voyage, he decided to instead seek the Northwest Passage. The ship reached eastern North America. While cruising along the Atlantic seaboard, Hudson entered a majestic river that Verrazzano had encountered in 1524. It was known from then on as the Hudson River. The expedition traveled up the river for about 150 miles (240 kilometers) to the vicinity of what is now Albany, New York. Hudson concluded that the river did not lead to the Pacific and began the return voyage.

The British East India Company and other English merchants sponsored Hudson's fourth and final voyage, to search for the Northwest Passage. This time he wanted to follow up on a report by the English explorer Captain George Weymouth regarding a possible channel to the Pacific. Weymouth had described an inlet—now named Hudson

A replica of Henry Hudson's ship, the *Half Moon,* sailed through New York Harbor at the mouth of the Hudson River in 2000.

Strait—where a "furious overfall" of water rushed out with every ebb tide. This phenomenon suggested that a great body of water lay beyond the strait. Hudson was confident that it was the Pacific Ocean.

Hudson sailed from London on April 17, 1610, in the *Discovery*. He proceeded to the "furious overfall," between Baffin Island and what is now northern Quebec. Passing through the strait, he entered the large inland sea that is now named Hudson Bay. He followed the east coast southward, reaching James Bay. With no outlet to the Pacific Ocean to be found, Hudson cruised aimlessly until winter overtook him.

In the close confinement of an Arctic winter, quarrels arose. Some crew members suspected that Hudson was secretly hoarding food for his favorites. On the homeward voyage, several of the crew rebelled. The mutineers seized Hudson, his son, and seven others, casting them adrift in Hudson Bay in a small

Henry Hudson was lost at sea in 1611 after members of his crew launched a mutiny and threw him and several others into a smaller boat.

open boat on June 22, 1611. The ringleaders and
several other crew members never returned home,
having been killed in a fight with Eskimos. Nothing
more was ever heard of Hudson and his small party.
His discoveries later formed the basis for the Dutch
colonization of the Hudson River and for English
claims to much of Canada.

CHAPTER FOUR

EXPLORING THE MISSISSIPPI

T he French colonial possessions in what are now Canada and the United States were known as New France. Much of New France was explored by fur traders, colonists, and especially Jesuit and Franciscan missionaries. The missionaries wanted to convert the Indians to Roman Catholicism. Most of the explorations were thus private undertakings. In 1672, however, the governor of New France sponsored an expedition to the Mississippi River. The explorers were to determine the direction of the

The pelts of the American beaver and other animals were one of the most valuable commodities traded in New France.

river's course and to find its mouth. The French hoped that the river emptied into the Pacific Ocean and would provide a passage to Asia.

JOLLIET AND MARQUETTE

The expedition was led by Louis Jolliet, who had studied to be a Jesuit but worked as a fur trader. His traveling companion was a Jesuit priest named Jacques Marquette. Marquette knew several Indian languages and served as an interpreter. The small party also included five other men.

On May 17, 1673, the expedition set out in two birchbark canoes from what is now St. Ignace, Michigan, for Green Bay, on Lake Michigan. The men then paddled up the Fox River in central Wisconsin and down the Wisconsin River. About a month later they entered the Mississippi River. The explorers traveled the great river's upper course, pausing along the way to make notes, to hunt, and to glean scraps of information from local Indians. Marquette also preached to the Indians he met.

In July the explorers arrived at a Quapaw Indian village at the mouth of the Arkansas River, about 40 miles (65 kilometers) north of what is now Arkansas City, Arkansas. From personal observations and from the friendly Quapaw, they concluded that the Mississippi flowed south into the Gulf of Mexico and not the Pacific. The river's mouth thus lay in the region held by the Spanish. Indians also warned

In 1673 Louis Jolliet and Jacques Marquette became the first Europeans to explore the upper reaches of the Mississippi River. Hernando de Soto had traveled the lower Mississippi more than a century earlier, in 1541.

that they would face hostile Indian tribes if they continued south. The party decided to return home, traveling back via the Illinois River and Green Bay. Although the explorers did not reach the mouth of the Mississippi, they reported the first accurate data on the river's upper course.

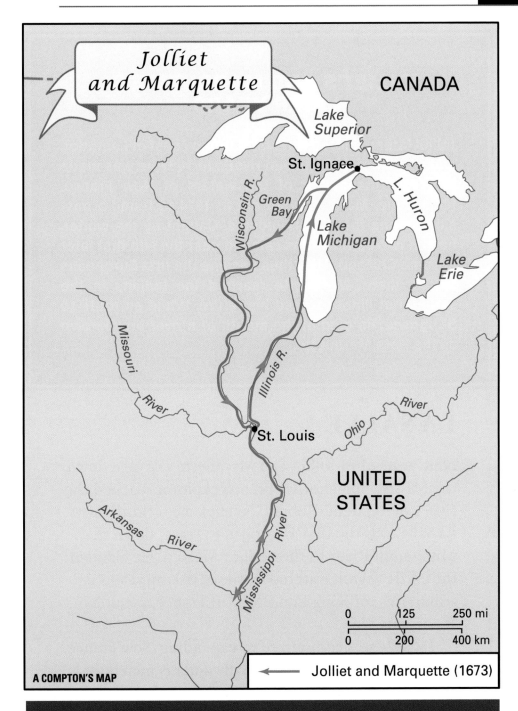

Jolliet
and Marquette

CANADA

Lake
Superior

St. Ignace

Wisconsin R.

Green
Bay

L. Huron

Lake
Michigan

Lake
Erie

Missouri

River

Illinois R.

River

St. Louis

Ohio

UNITED
STATES

Arkansas

River

Mississippi River

0   125   250 mi
0   200   400 km

A COMPTON'S MAP

⟵   Jolliet and Marquette (1673)

Map of Jolliet and Marquette's journey from Lake Michigan to the
Arkansas River.

JOLLIET'S AND MARQUETTE'S LATER YEARS

Jolliet later explored Hudson Bay, the coast of Labrador, and a number of Canadian rivers. In 1697 he was made the royal mapmaker of the waters of New France. Meanwhile, Marquette set out in 1674 to found a mission among the Illinois Indians. Caught by the winter, he and two companions camped near the site that later became Chicago. They thus became the first Europeans to live there. Marquette reached the Indians in the spring, but illness forced his return. While en route to St. Ignace, he died at the mouth of a river now known as the Père Marquette.

LA SALLE

Nine years after Jolliet and Marquette's voyage down the Mississippi, another French explorer reached the river's delta. René-Robert Cavelier, sieur (lord) de La Salle, was the first European to travel down the Mississippi River to the Gulf of Mexico. He claimed the entire region watered by the Mississippi and its tributaries for King Louis XIV of France, naming it "Louisiana."

La Salle was committed to expanding New France. In the winter of 1678–79 La Salle and his men built a fort at the Niagara River. There they built a 40-ton

(36-tonne) ship, the *Griffon*. La Salle's lieutenant was Henri de Tonty, an Italian adventurer. The Indians called Tonty the "man with the iron hand" because he had a metal claw replacing a hand blown off in battle.

On August 7, 1679, the expedition set sail. The explorers reached Green Bay in September and sent the ship back laden with furs. It was never heard from again. Early in 1680 the explorers built Fort Crèvecoeur near what is now Peoria, Illinois. From this fort La Salle sent Louis Hennepin, a Franciscan friar, with two companions to explore the upper Mississippi.

Leaving Tonty in charge of the new fort, La Salle made a trip to another French fort for supplies. On his return, he learned that the Iroquois had destroyed Fort Crèvecoeur. Tonty and his men had vanished. La Salle traced them northward, meeting up with them in what is now Mackinaw City, Michigan.

Early in 1682 La Salle and Tonty finally set out again for the Mississippi River. They canoed down the Illinois River and the Mississippi, reaching the Gulf of Mexico on April 9. La Salle claimed the Mississippi Valley for France. Within a generation, the Mississippi became a vital link between French settlements along the Gulf of Mexico and in Canada.

In 1684 La Salle made one more voyage to the Mississippi. He wanted to build fortified colonies at the river's mouth and to conquer part of the Spanish

René-Robert Cavelier, sieur de La Salle, claimed the entire Mississippi River valley for France under the name of Louisiana.

province of Mexico. This expedition was doomed from the start. Vessels were lost by piracy and shipwreck, and sickness took a heavy toll of the colonists. Finally, a gross miscalculation brought the ships to Matagorda Bay in Texas, 500 miles (800 kilometers) west of their intended landfall. After several fruitless journeys in search of his lost Mississippi, La Salle was murdered by some of his men near the Brazos River.

CONCLUSION

O nce European powers had established their claims in North America, they sent wave after wave of settlers to establish colonies there. This marked the end of the Age of Exploration and the beginning of the colonial era. However, the exploration of North America was still not complete. Early settlements were primarily clustered along the coasts or the St. Lawrence River, and though the colonists gradually moved inland, they continued to regard most of the landmass of what is now the United States as an uncharted wilderness. By the time that the 13 Colonies broke away from England to form the United States, there remained vast swaths of the continent about which the inhabitants of the new nation knew little to nothing.

The first Americans to explore the area west of the Mississippi were Meriwether Lewis and William Clark. Between 1804 and 1806 their famous expedition traveled from the Mississippi River to the Pacific coast and back. Their expedition contributed significant geographic and scientific knowledge of the West, aided the expansion of the fur trade, and strengthened U.S. claims to the Pacific. The

Captai

ewis & Clark holding a Council with the Indians   Page 17

This illustration shows Lewis and Clark meeting with a group of Native Americans. It comes from an account of the voyage that was based on expedition member Sergeant Patrick Gass's diary and published in 1810.

expedition was soon followed by the mountain men, pioneers who went to the Rocky Mountain region first as fur trappers to obtain beaver pelts. The most experienced trappers were the French, who were joined by American and Spanish fur traders. Mingling extensively with the Indians, the mountain men adopted many of their manners of life and their beliefs. Like all of the explorers who came before, these bold adventurers paved the way for settlers who would bring sweeping changes to the land.

TIMELINE

1492 Christopher Columbus lands in the Caribbean islands on October 12.

1493 Pope Alexander VI establishes the Line of Demarcation about 320 miles (515 kilometers) west of the Cape Verde Islands, settling a dispute between Spain and Portugal.

1494 Spain and Portugal negotiate a treaty that moves the Line of Demarcation to about 1,185 miles (1,900 kilometers) west of the Cape Verde Islands.

1497 John Cabot lands in what is now Canada and claims the land there for England.

1500 Pedro Álvares Cabral lands in Brazil and claims it for Portugal.

1513 Juan Ponce de León becomes the first European to visit what is now Florida.

1520 Magellan's expedition makes it through the Strait of Magellan and into the Pacific Ocean.

1524 Giovanni da Verrazzano reaches Cape Fear (in what is now North Carolina) and sails north up the coast.

1534 Jacques Cartier explores the Gulf of St. Lawrence on an expedition for King Francis I of France.

1540 Francisco Vázquez de Coronado sets off in search of the Seven Cities of Cíbola.

1541 Hernando de Soto and his men become the first Europeans to travel on the Mississippi River.

1587   Settlers recruited by Sir Walter Raleigh establish the first English colony in North America on Roanoke Island, in what is now North Carolina. By August 1590 the settlers had disappeared.

1607   Jamestown, the first permanent English colony in America, is founded on a peninsula of the James River in what is now Virginia.

1608   Samuel de Champlain founds Quebec city, France's first permanent colony in the Americas.

1609   Henry Hudson, sailing for the Dutch East India Company, explores the eastern coast of North America. He sails up the Hudson River as far as present-day Albany, New York.

1673   A small party led by Louis Jolliet and Jacques Marquette explores the Mississippi River between the Wisconsin River and the mouth of the Arkansas River in what is now Arkansas.

1682   René-Robert Cavelier, sieur de La Salle, sails down the Mississippi River to the Gulf of Mexico.

GLOSSARY

caravel A light sailing ship of the 15th, 16th, and 17th centuries in Europe, much-used by the Spanish and Portuguese for long voyages.

cartographer A person who makes maps.

colonize To send settlers to new territory that a country or other power has taken control of.

commission To ask or order someone to carry out a specific task.

comrade A close friend or associate; companion.

elusive Hard to find or capture.

embellish To make something more interesting by adding details.

expedition A journey or trip undertaken for a specific purpose (as war or exploring).

exploit To get value or use from.

globalization The development of economic and cultural links throughout the world.

hoard To build up and not share a hidden supply of something.

maritime Having to do with the sea.

monopoly Complete control over the entire supply of goods or a service in a certain market.

mutineer A person guilty of mutiny, which is a rebellion against the officer in charge.

navigator A person who is responsible for directing the course of a ship or aircraft.

Northwest Passage A sea route from the Atlantic Ocean to the Pacific Ocean that goes through Canada's Arctic islands.

overland By, on, or across land.

peninsula A piece of land that is nearly surrounded by water and is attached to a larger land area.

phenomenon An observable fact or event; a fact, feature, or event of scientific interest.

plantation An agricultural estate usually worked by resident laborers.

strait A narrow passage of water that connects two large bodies of water.

tributary A stream flowing into a larger stream or a lake.

venture An undertaking involving chance, risk, or danger.

Canadian Museum of History
100 Rue Laurier
Gatineau, QC K1A 0M8
Canada
(819) 776-7000
Website: http://www.historymuseum.ca/home
While this museum, the country's most visited, has
roots reaching back to the mid-19th century, its
present building dates from 1989. The museum's
excellent online Virtual Museum of New France
offers a wealth of information about the French
explorers and settlers of Canada.

Cartier-Brébeuf National Historic Site
175 Rue de l'Espinay
Quebec, QC G1L 3W6
Canada
(418) 648-7016
Website: http://www.pc.gc.ca/eng/lhn-nhs/qc/cartier-
brebeuf/index.aspx
This park commemorates the winter of 1535–36, which
Cartier and his men spent in the Iroquois village of
Stadacona, as well as the residence of the first Jesuit
missionaries who settled in Quebec in 1625–26.
Visitors can appreciate the site's natural beauty or
take part in an educational program.

Historic Jamestowne
1368 Colonial National Historic Parkway
Jamestown, VA 23081
(757) 856-1250
Website: http://historicjamestowne.org
Visitors can learn about the first permanent English
    settlement in North America at this cultural her-
    itage site. There are reconstructed buildings and
    reenactors showing how the English colonists
    lived. The ongoing archaeological excavations at
    the James Fort site continue to produce interesting
    new finds.

The Mariners' Museum and Park
100 Museum Drive
Newport News, VA 23606
(757) 596-2222
Website: http://www.marinersmuseum.org
Dedicated to spreading an appreciation of maritime
    history and culture, this museum's collection
    includes navigation and scientific instruments, ship
    models, figureheads, paintings, maps, photographs,
    and more. The Mariners' Museum Library and
    Archives, now housed at the nearby Christopher
    Newport University, has the largest maritime collec-
    tion in the Western Hemisphere.

New Netherland Institute
P.O. Box 2536

Empire State Plaza
Albany, NY 12220
(518) 486-4815
Website: http://www.newnetherlandinstitute.org
Founded in 1986, this institute educates the public
about the role that the Dutch played in the exploration, settlement, and development of North
America. Its support has enabled the translation,
transcription, and study of Dutch records from the
17th century.

Rare Book and Special Collections Division
Library of Congress
101 Independence Avenue SE
Washington, DC 20540
(202) 707-3448
Website: http://www.loc.gov/rr/rarebook
This branch of the national library of the United States
has many priceless documents related to American
history. These include the materials in the Jay I.
Kislak Collection, which focuses on early American
history and the cultures of Florida, Mesoamerica,
and the Caribbean.

Roanoke Adventure Museum
1 Festival Park
Manteo, NC 27954
(252) 475-1500
Website: http://roanokeisland.com/
RoanokeAdventureMuseum.aspx

Visitors can learn about the mysterious lost Roanoke colony and the lives of the English people who settled there. There are also exhibits about the subsequent history of the Outer Banks.

Texas State Library and Historical Commission
1201 Brazos Street
Austin, TX 78701
(512) 463-5455
Website: https://www.tsl.texas.gov
The commission oversees the state's library system and its archives. The Texas State Archives contain not just a vast array of government documents but also a wealth of historical maps, newspapers, broadsides, photographs, journals, and more.

WEBSITES

Due to the changing nature of Internet links, Rosen Publishing has developed an online list of websites related to the subject of this book. This sire is updated regularly. Please use this link to access the list:

http://www.rosenlinks.com/EAH/Exp

BIBLIOGRAPHY

Bader, Bonnie. *Who Was Christopher Columbus?* New York, NY: Grosset & Dunlap, 2013.

Blake, John. *The Sea Chart: The Illustrated History of Nautical Maps and Navigational Charts*. Annapolis, MD: Naval Institute Press, 2009.

Brunelle, Gayle K., ed. *Samuel de Champlain: Founder of New France*. Boston, MA: Bedford/St. Martin's, 2012.

Krull, Kathleen. *Lives of the Explorers: Discoveries, Disasters (and What the Neighbors Thought)*. Boston, MA: Houghton Mifflin Harcourt, 2014.

Lacoursière, Jacques, and Robin Philpot. *A People's History of Quebec*. Montreal, QC: Baraka Books, 2009.

Matthews, Rupert. *Explorer*. Revised edition. (DK Eyewitness Books). New York, NY: DK Children, 2012.

Mooney, Carla. *Explorers of the New World: Discover the Golden Age of Exploration*. White River Junction, VT: Nomad Press, 2011.

O'Brien, Patrick. *Atlas of World History*. 2nd edition. New York, NY: Oxford University Press; 2010.

Pletcher, Kenneth, ed. *The Age of Exploration: From Christopher Columbus to Ferdinand Magellan*. New York, NY: Britannica Educational Publishing, 2013.

Ross, Stewart. *Into the Unknown: How Great Explorers Found Their Way by Land, Sea, and Air*. Somerville, MA: Candlewick Press, 2014.

INDEX